W9-AUU-945

Date: 3/6/18

**J 599.86 MER
Merwin, E.,
Snub-nosed monkey /**

Snub-Nosed Monkey

by E. Merwin

Consultant: Darin Collins, DVM
Director, Animal Health Programs
Woodland Park Zoo
Seattle, Washington

BEARPORT
PUBLISHING

New York, New York

Credits

Cover, © Thomas Marent/Minden Pictures; TOC, © Zeng Wei Jun/Shutterstock; 4–5, © Thomas Marent/Minden Pictures; 6, © Wang LiQiang/Shutterstock; 7, © Stephen Belcher/Minden Pictures; 8, © Brian Kinney/Shutterstock; 9T, © Xi Zhinong/NPL/Minden Pictures; 9B, © Wang LiQiang/Shutterstock; 10, © Ricardas Anusauskas/Alamy Stock Photo; 11, © Thomas Marent/Minden Pictures; 12–13, © Wang LiQiang/Shutterstock; 13T, © Liqiang Wang/Dreamstime; 13B, © blickwinkel/Lundqvist/Alamy Stock Photo; 14T, © Paul Reeves Photography/Shutterstock; 14B, © Kevin Schafer/Alamy Stock Photo; 15, © pkujiahe/iStock; 16L, © Cyril Ruoso/Minden Pictures; 16–17, © Thomas Marent/Minden Pictures; 18T, © Valery Shanin/Shutterstock; 18B, © Staffan Widstrand/Nature Picture Library/Alamy Stock Photo; 19, © Xi Zhinong/Minden Pictures; 20L, © Cyril Ruoso/Minden Pictures; 20–21, © Florian Mollers/NPL/Minden Pictures; 22 (T to B), © hallam creations/Shutterstock, © cicloco/iStock, and © kjorgen/iStock; 23TL, © Wang LiQiang/Shutterstock; 23TR, © pixelrain/Shutterstock; 23BL, © Bree Herbert/Shutterstock; 23BR, © Wang LiQiang/Shutterstock; Back Cover, © Plovema/Dreamstime.

Publisher: Kenn Goin
Senior Editor: Joyce Tavolacci
Creative Director: Spencer Brinker
Design: Debrah Kaiser

Library of Congress Cataloging-in-Publication Data in process at time of publication (2018)
Library of Congress Control Number: 2017007489
ISBN-13: 978-1-68402-263-2 (library binding)

For more information, write to Bearport Publishing Company, Inc., 45 West 21st Street, Suite 3B, New York, New York 10010. Printed in the United States of America.

10 9 8 7 6 5 4 3 2 1

Contents

What's this weird but cute animal?

Fuzzy fur!

It's a **snub-nosed monkey.**

Bluish face!

PUSHED-IN nose!

5

Snub-nosed monkeys live in mountain forests in Asia.

Brrr! Brrr! In the winter, it can get very cold.

The monkeys' thick, fuzzy fur keeps them warm.

Even the monkeys' hands are furry. It looks as if they're wearing mittens!

These fuzzy monkeys have teeny, flat noses.

No one is sure why.

Some **experts** think a bigger nose might freeze off in the icy weather.

golden snub-nosed monkey

gray snub-nosed monkey

black snub-nosed monkey

There are five different kinds of snub-nosed monkeys. Each one has a short, flat nose.

9

Check out this black snub-nosed monkey's plump lips.

As the males grow up, their lips balloon out.

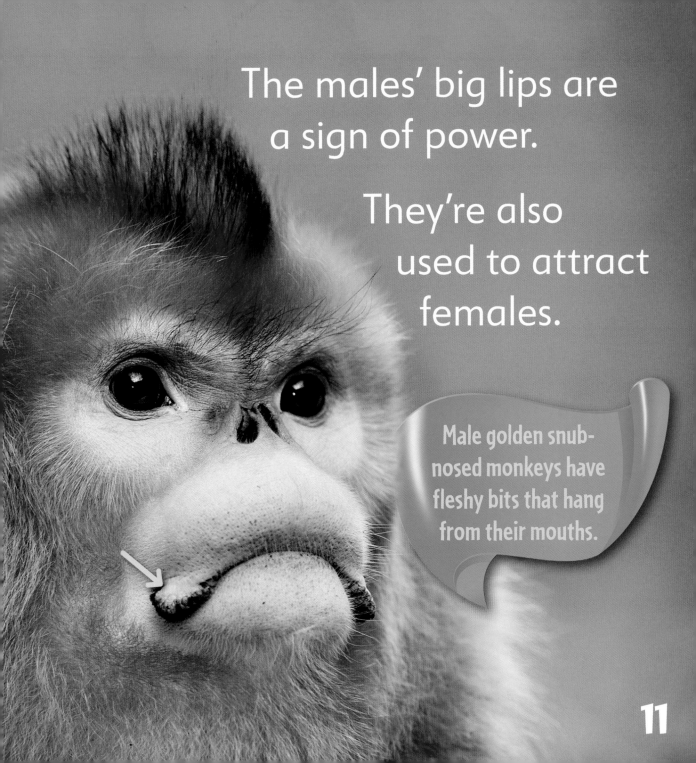

The males' big lips are a sign of power.

They're also used to attract females.

Male golden snub-nosed monkeys have fleshy bits that hang from their mouths.

Belch, moan, hoot, and holler!

Snub-nosed monkeys make about 18 different sounds.

These sounds help them **communicate** with other monkeys.

Snub-nosed monkeys can make sounds without moving their lips!

13

Watch out!

These monkeys have many enemies.

Eagles attack from the air.

Wild dogs hunt them on the ground.

Young males hang out in groups. They're on the lookout for danger!

Don't mess with this monkey's large family!

If an enemy comes too close, the monkeys swing into action.

Hundreds will fight to **protect** the group.

When there's danger, females stand side-by-side. They make a wall to protect their babies.

Tasty berries!

Crunchy seeds!

Leaves and **lichen**!

lichen

Snub-nosed monkeys find lots of food to eat in the forest.

In winter, the monkeys eat mostly tree bark.

19

After eating, it's time
to sleep.

On a low branch, a
group of monkeys cuddle.

They keep each other warm
through the cold night.

Snub-nosed monkeys can live for more than 20 years.

More Weird Monkeys

De Brazza's Monkey

This monkey has an orange patch of fur above its eyes. It also has a long, white beard that makes it look like an old man!

Howler Monkey

A howler monkey is one of the loudest animals in the world. The monkey's booming hoots and howls can be heard 3 miles (4.8 km) away!

Proboscis Monkey

A proboscis (proh-BOHS-is) monkey has a huge, droopy nose that can grow to be 7 inches (18 cm) long! These animals can also outswim a crocodile.

Glossary

communicate
(kuh-MYOO-nuh-kayt)
to pass on information,
ideas, or feelings

experts (EK-spurts)
people who know a lot
about something

lichen (LYE-kuhn) flat
plant-like living things
that grow on rocks
and trees

protect (pro-TEKT)
to keep something
safe

Index

Read More

Neuman, Susan B. *Hang On, Monkey!* Washington, DC: National Geographic (2014).

Schreiber, Anne. *Monkeys.* Washington, DC: National Geographic (2013).

Learn More Online

To learn more about snub-nosed monkeys, visit
www.bearportpublishing.com/WeirderAndCuter

About the Author

E. Merwin writes stories, poems, and books for kids and adults. As a primate herself, she much admires the snub-nosed monkey and the kindness and care of the animal experts in Asia who are working to keep this endangered species alive.